50 YEARS AGO IN NEW YORK, A MAN NAMED CRAZY JOE GALLO WAS MURDERED. YOUR MISSION IS TO PREVENT HIS MURDER.

I CAN'T BELIEVE MY EARS!

CRAZY JOE WAS AN ITALIAN AMERICAN MOBSTER, A 'CAPO REGIME' IN THE COLUMBO FAMILY... BY 1972 HE WAS DIAGNOSED AS A DANGEROUS SCHIZOPHRENIC.

GALLO, THEY SAY, MURDERED ALBERT ANASTASIA... ONE OCTOBER DAY, HE WAS LEFT SHIRTLESS AND DEAD.

HE IS ONE OF THE 27-YEAR-OLDS WE WANT BACK ASAP! HENDRIX IS ON THAT LIST

MY MISSION WITH CRAZY JOEY GALLO HAS BEEN ACCOMPLISHED... I WILL TAKE ON THE MISSION ACHILLES - TRIBECA IS FIRST!

OF COURSE, WHO DOESN'T REMEMBER MORRISON... IS THAT WHO YOU'RE TALKING ABOUT ACHILLES?

...SOMETHING THAT RESEMBLES A BETRAYAL, CAN BE RESOLVED WITH COMFORT... GO BOSS ANGEL AND WISH YOU LUCK!

BOSS ANGEL IS CONTEMPLATING TELLING DYLAN THE COMPLETE STORY...

BOSS ANGEL, I BET YOU'RE WONDERING HY YOU'VE ARRIVED HERE IN FLORIDA?
SAFE TO SAY YOU'VE BEEN FULL OF SURPRISES DURING MY HALF STEP INTO HEAVEN! WHEN WILL THE PEARLY GATES OPEN FOR ME?
I DON'T HAVE AN ANSWER FOR THAT. BUT RIGHT NOW, YOU HAVE ANOTHER SAVE TO MAK
DO YOU KNOW WHO JIM MORRISON IS?

MORRISON WAS A GREAT AMERICAN ROCK'N'ROLL SINGER SAID TO BE AMONGST THE BEST MUSICIANS OF HIS TIME. HIS MUSIC AND WILD LIFESTYLE MADE HIM THE TALK OF THE NATION

A SECOND CHANCE FOR THE KING OF ROCK. THIS COULD BE HIS SHOT AT REDEMPTION.

"THANKS, BOSS ANGEL. YOU'VE REKINDLED A FRIENDSHIP THAT WAS LOST TO TIME."

"I DID WHAT I COULD. I HOPE HE MAKES THE MOST OF THIS SECOND CHANCE."

AND SO, THE SAVIOUR FADES INTO OBLIV[ION], LEAVING BEHIND A TALE OF REDEMPTION, FRIENDSHIP AND ROCK N' ROLL.

www.ingramcontent.com/pod-product-compliance
Lightning Source LLC
LaVergne TN
LVHW072132060526
838201LV00072B/5020